The Best 50

SUNDAE RECIPES

Nancy Root Miller

BRISTOL PUBLISHING ENTERPRISES
Hayward, California

Printed in the United States of America.
ISBN: 1-55867-317-2
Cover design: Frank J. Paredes
Cover photography: John A. Benson
Recipe consultant: Randy Mon

THE PERFECT ICE CREAM DESSERT!

Begin with the ice cream, cold and smooth, flavors melting on your tongue. Then a dense fudge sauce adding a burst of chocolate. Next, airy whipped cream, simultaneously light and rich. Add a contrasting crunch of nuts, crown the concoction with a cherry and you have a perfect ice cream sundae.

Today, with the variety of ice cream flavors and toppings available in the average supermarket, sundaes can be anything you want them to be, from fabulously decadent to downright healthy.

THE ORIGIN OF THE SUNDAE

Although we have loved ice cream for centuries, the sundae as we know it has only been around for a little over a hundred years. My home state of Wisconsin lays claim to the first ice cream sundae. Before 1881, the main alternative to a bowl of ice cream was the soda: carbonated water, a squirt of chocolate sauce, and a scoop of ice cream. But conservative church elders found "sucking soda" to be too frivolous a pastime on the Lord's day, and banned sodas on Sundays. As the story goes, a customer walked into Ed Berners' ice cream parlor in the town of Two Rivers one summer day in 1881 and requested an ice cream soda. Since it was the Sabbath, Mr. Berners, a fast-thinking guy, prepared a dish of ice cream topped with chocolate sauce but omitted the forbidden fizzy water. His creation caught on and became a regular Sunday treat. One weekday a young girl asked for ice cream with "that stuff on top, that you only serve on Sundays." Thus was born the "sunday." But religious leaders found the name sacrilegious, so the spelling was changed to "sundi," "sondhi," and eventually stuck at "sundae."

But is this the true origin of the sundae? While experts generally agree on the circumstances, the location is in dispute. In addition to Two Rivers, Wisconsin, nearby Manitowoc, Wisconsin also lays claim to serving the first sundae, as do Ithaca and Buffalo, New

York; Evanston and Plainfield, Illinois; and Norfolk, Virginia. In addition, Latrobe, Pennsylvania and Wilmington, Ohio are battling over the first-time rights to the banana split. We may never know which shop owner and patron were responsible for the sundae, but whoever they are, they have our undying gratitude.

THE MODERN SUNDAE

The sundae has come a long way since its hotly debated origins. The basic concept of vanilla ice cream topped with chocolate sauce, although still delicious, has been expanded to encompass a world of flavors and textures.

While classic vanilla is hard to beat for its simplicity and adaptability to myriad toppings, the sky's the limit when it comes to ice cream. Think of chocolate ice cream with peanut butter topping, peach ice cream with raspberry puree, or maple walnut ice cream with cinnamon apple topping. Whatever your favorite flavor, there's a topping — or several — that will complement it.

Is ice cream a bit heavy for you? Try sherbet or frozen yogurt, both lower in fat than premium ice cream. In the United States, sherbet is usually made from a mixture of sweetened fruit and milk, although it can be made simply with fruit and sugar. Frozen yogurt is often, but not always, made with live active yogurt cultures that aid in digestion. But if a healthy diet is a concern, read the label — double chocolate candy bar crunch frozen yogurt may have more fat and calories than plain vanilla ice cream.

For a frozen treat that is nearly or completely fat free, try sorbet. This luscious concoction is far lighter than ice cream, but smoother and creamier than Italian ice. It is usually made with a fruit puree or fruit juice combined with a sugar syrup. It's quite simple to prepare, and can be made with or without an ice cream maker. See the *Sorbets* in this book, pages 35–45. If you're making it at home, and only adults will be eating it, add a tablespoon or two of a complementary liqueur, or even vodka. Since alcohol won't freeze at standard home freezer temperatures, a small amount will keep your sorbet softer in texture.

Ice cream alone — or frozen yogurt, or sherbet, or sorbet — does not a sundae make. Sauces range from the utterly decadent like *Chocolate Butterscotch Peanut Butter Sauce*, page 62, to the light and, dare we say it, healthy *Cherry Blackberry Sauce*, page 52, or *Tangy Lemon Sauce*, page 57. Let the combination suit your mood. Strawberry sherbet can be virtuously paired with *Blueberry Sauce*, page 53, or extravagantly topped with rich *Classic Chocolate Sauce*, page 58. Or try a combination of sauces, such as chocolate and raspberry sauces together, or strawberry and lemon. Kids always love marshmallow creme straight from a jar, ladled over ice cream and topped with a cherry.

A perfect sundae can easily be created with a frozen treat and a sauce. But for those times when you just need a little more, consider adding a topping or a base. Whipped cream is of course the first topping to come to mind, perhaps with the addition of a maraschino cherry. Nuts are another logical choice, but don't limit yourself to walnuts or pecans; how about pistachios, or macadamias, or even pine nuts? Crumbled cookies will add crunch, as will crushed candy canes. Armed with a vegetable peeler and a bar of chocolate, you can top a sundae with elegant chocolate curls in a moment. And a simple scattering of fresh berries will lighten up almost any sundae. The *Accompaniments* section of this book, pages 66–76, offers recipes for a number of delicate cookies that can be inserted in the top of a sundae for a final flourish.

We've taken care of the top; now let's see what could be underneath. A banana split starts with halved bananas. What about a base of poached pear or peach halves? Add a scoop of vanilla ice cream and a drizzle of raspberry sauce and you have a dessert fit for a sophisticated dinner party. Or start with a brownie, add butter pecan ice cream and top it with caramel sauce — fabulous! Our *S'mores Sundae*, page 17, starts with, obviously, a graham cracker. Instead of a waffle cone for your ice cream, start with a toasted waffle while building your sundae.

Sundaes are not just for dessert. The *Healthy Sundaes* section, pages 46–51, contains recipes for yogurt- and fruit-based sundaes perfect for breakfast or an after-school snack.

A sundae party may be the easiest and most popular method of entertaining. Just about all of the sauces in this book can be made ahead and reheated in the microwave, so all your preparation can be done up to a few days before the event. Set out several types of ice cream, a number of sauces, and bowls of assorted toppings. Give a prize for the most creative sundae. Hot sauces can be kept warm in non-electric fondue pots, and ice cream containers can be placed in large bowls of ice. Add bowls, spoons, and a pile of napkins and you're ready to go.

Following, you'll find more than fifty fabulous recipes to set you on the road to sundae enlightenment. But feel free to create your own unique combinations. After all, sundaes are the ultimate form of gratification. Enjoy!

COFFEE BROWNIE SUNDAE

This is a simple way to treat a crowd with fabulous sundaes: the brownie can be made a few days ahead. For more chocolate heaven, stir 1/2 cup chocolate chips into brownie batter before baking.

3/4 cup flour
1/2 tsp. baking powder
1/2 tsp. salt
1/2 cup (1 stick) butter, chopped
2 oz. unsweetened chocolate, coarsely chopped
1 tbs. instant coffee or instant espresso powder
1 tbs. hot water
1 cup sugar
2 eggs
1/2 gal. vanilla ice cream
1/2 gal. coffee ice cream
3 cups prepared chocolate sauce

Heat oven to 350°. Butter a 12-inch round pizza pan. In a small bowl, stir together flour, baking powder and salt; set aside. Place butter and chocolate in a glass bowl and microwave on high for 1 minute. Remove, stir, and microwave in 30-second increments, stirring after each round, until just melted. Stir until smooth and set aside.

Place coffee and water in a medium bowl and stir until dissolved. Stir in sugar, then beat in eggs. Stir in flour mixture until just combined. Spread batter in prepared pizza pan and bake for about 15 minutes or until brownie just pulls away from the sides of the pan. Cool in pan.

Cut brownie into 12 wedges. Top each wedge with a small scoop each of vanilla and coffee ice cream and drizzle with chocolate sauce.

BANANA SPLIT

Makes 4 servings

How about chocolate, butter pecan, and maple walnut ice creams? Or three kinds of fruit sherbets? It's up to you!

1 cup fresh raspberries
3 tbs. sugar, divided
1/2 cup heavy cream
4 small bananas
4 cups ice cream (any flavor)

1/2 cup crushed pineapple in
  syrup, drained
3/4 cup chocolate sauce
1/2 cup toasted walnuts, optional
4 maraschino cherries

In a small bowl, mash raspberries with 2 tbs. of the sugar; set aside. In a separate bowl, beat cream with remaining 1 tbs. sugar until soft peaks form; set aside. Peel bananas and halve lengthwise. Place 2 halves in each serving bowl and top each bowl with 3 small scoops ice cream. Spoon reserved raspberries over 1 scoop, pineapple over another scoop, and drizzle remaining scoop with chocolate sauce. Garnish with whipped cream and nuts, if desired, and top each sundae with a cherry.

COCONUT COFFEE CHOCOLATE SUNDAE

Makes 4 servings

Coffee and chocolate, yes. Chocolate and coconut, of course. But all three together? Try it, and you'll wonder why you didn't think of it long ago.

$1/2$ cup shredded coconut
$1/2$ cup heavy cream
1 cup semisweet chocolate
  chips

2 tbs. coffee liqueur
1 pt. coffee ice cream

Place coconut in a small skillet over medium-low heat and toast until light golden and fragrant. Set aside. (You could also toast the coconut in a 350° oven for 8 to 10 minutes.)

Place cream and chocolate chips in a glass bowl and microwave on high 1 minute. Stir and microwave in 30-second increments until just melted. Stir until smooth. Stir in liqueur.

Place 1 scoop ice cream in each serving bowl. Top with warm chocolate sauce and sprinkle with toasted coconut.

SUPER MINT CHOCOLATE SUNDAE

Makes 4 servings

This mint-lover's sundae has that pungent herb in every layer. To lessen the impact, use chocolate ice cream instead of mint chip.

1 cup plus 1 1/2 tbs. sugar, divided
1 cup water
1/2 cup thinly sliced fresh mint, or 2 mint tea bags
2/3 cup unsweetened cocoa powder

1/4 cup (1/2 stick) butter, softened
1 cup heavy cream
1/4 tsp. peppermint extract
1 pt. mint chocolate chip ice cream

Place 1 cup of the sugar and water in a small saucepan over high heat and bring to a boil. Boil for 1 minute. Pour into a bowl and stir in mint leaves (or place tea bags in syrup). Set aside for 1 hour to steep.

Strain syrup into a medium saucepan and whisk in cocoa powder. Place over medium heat and bring to a boil, whisking often. Boil, whisking, for 1 minute or until sauce is smooth. Whisk in butter until butter is melted and sauce is smooth. Refrigerate sauce to allow it to thicken.

In a large bowl, using an electric mixer, beat cream with remaining $1\frac{1}{2}$ tbs. sugar until slightly thickened. Add peppermint extract and continue beating until soft peaks form.

Place 1 scoop ice cream in each serving dish. Drizzle with chocolate mint sauce, and top with mint whipped cream.

WHITE CHOCOLATE COCONUT SUNDAE

Chocolate and coconut have always been a happy combination; white chocolate adds an extra dimension. Macadamia nuts would be a fitting addition, if you so desire.

1/3 cup shredded coconut
6 oz. white chocolate, chopped
1/3 cup heavy cream

2 tbs. light rum, or 1/2 tsp. rum extract
2 pt. coconut ice cream

Heat oven to 350°. Spread coconut on a cookie sheet and toast for 8 to 10 minutes until light golden. Set aside. (You could also toast the coconut in a skillet over medium-low heat until golden.)

Place chocolate in a glass bowl and microwave on high 1 minute. Stir, and microwave in 30-second increments, stirring after each round, until just melted. Stir until smooth. Whisk in cream and rum and refrigerate until ready to use.

Place 2 small scoops ice cream in each serving dish. Top with white chocolate sauce and sprinkle with toasted coconut.

PEANUT BUTTER CHOCOLATE SUNDAE

Makes 4 servings

This peanut butter sauce couldn't be easier. Try this sundae topped with sliced bananas or chopped peanuts as well.

$1/2$ cup water
$3/4$ cup sugar
$1/2$ cup peanut butter

1 bar chocolate (about 2 oz.)
1 pt. chocolate ice cream

Place water and sugar in a small saucepan over medium-high heat. Bring to a boil, stirring occasionally. Boil until all sugar is dissolved, then continue to boil 1 minute longer. Remove from heat and stir in peanut butter. Using an electric mixer, beat until smooth.

Use a vegetable peeler to "peel" curls of chocolate from the chocolate bar. Set curls aside.

Place 1 scoop ice cream in each serving dish. Top with warm peanut butter sauce, and garnish with chocolate curls.

ROCKY ROAD SUNDAE

Classic rocky road ice cream gets deconstructed into a sundae. Use vanilla ice cream instead of chocolate, if you wish, and almonds or pecans instead of walnuts. Make sure your marshmallows are fresh: stale marshmallows won't melt well.

1/3 cup heavy cream
1 cup (6 oz.) dark chocolate chips
1 cup mini marshmallows,
   divided

1/2 cup chopped walnuts,
   toasted, divided
1 pt. chocolate ice cream
whipped cream for garnish

Place cream, chocolate chips and 1/2 cup of the marshmallows in a glass bowl and microwave on high 1 minute. Stir, and microwave in 30-second increments, stirring after each round, until just melted. Stir until smooth. Stir in 1/4 cup of the walnuts.

Place 1 scoop ice cream in each serving dish. Top with warm sauce. Sprinkle with remaining 1/4 cup walnuts and remaining 1/2 cup marshmallows, and top with whipped cream.

S'MORES SUNDAE

No campfire handy? Make these classic treats at home. A scoop of ice cream only makes s'mores better.

Classic Chocolate Sauce, page 58
8 large marshmallows
8 squares graham crackers
1 pt. vanilla or chocolate ice cream

Heat chocolate sauce in microwave for 1 minute or until warm; set aside. Thread 2 marshmallows onto each of 4 skewers and toast them over a gas or electric burner on high until golden (don't let the marshmallows touch the burners). Place 1 graham cracker in the bottom of each serving dish. Top with a scoop of ice cream, and drizzle chocolate sauce over top. Coarsely crumble remaining crackers over chocolate sauce. Garnish with warm marshmallow skewers.

NEW ORLEANS PECAN SUNDAE

Caramel and pecan-studded pralines, a Louisiana favorite, take the form of a luscious sundae. Try with butter-pecan ice cream.

2 tbs. butter
$1/2$ cup brown sugar, packed
6 large marshmallows
1 tbs. light corn syrup
1 pinch salt
$1/2$ cup evaporated milk

$1/2$ tsp. vanilla
$1/2$ cup chopped pecans
1 pt. vanilla ice cream
$1/2$ cup pecan halves
whipped cream for garnish

Melt butter in a small saucepan over medium-low heat. Stir in brown sugar, marshmallows, corn syrup and salt. Cook, stirring constantly, until mixture comes to a boil and sauce is smooth. Boil for 1 minute and remove from heat. Stir in evaporated milk, vanilla and chopped pecans. Place 1 scoop of ice cream in each serving bowl. Top with warm caramel-pecan sauce. Garnish with pecan halves and whipped cream.

CHOCOLATE RASPBERRY WAFFLE SUNDAE   Makes 4 servings

Ordinary frozen waffles are magically transformed into a lavish dessert. For homemade chocolate sauce recipes, see pages 58–62.

2 cups fresh raspberries, or
  frozen unsweetened, thawed
1/4 cup sugar, or to taste
1/4 cup water
1 cup prepared chocolate sauce

4 frozen waffles
1 pt. ice cream (vanilla,
  chocolate or raspberry)
whipped cream for garnish
fresh raspberries for garnish

Place raspberries, sugar and water in a medium saucepan over medium-low heat. Bring to a simmer and cook 5 minutes, until sauce is thick and berries begin to break down. Set aside to cool slightly. Heat chocolate sauce for 1 minute in microwave, if desired.

Follow directions on the box to toast waffles. Place 1 waffle on each dessert plate. Add a scoop of ice cream. Spoon raspberry sauce over ice cream, and drizzle with chocolate sauce. Garnish with whipped cream and a few fresh raspberries.

WHITE CHOCOLATE
STRAWBERRY SUNDAE

Think of a chocolate-dipped strawberry in the form of a sundae. The white chocolate sauce and strawberries can be prepared up to a day ahead and refrigerated; just give the chocolate sauce a good whisk before serving.

1 pt. fresh strawberries, hulled and quartered
3 tbs. confectioners' sugar
2 tbs. framboise (raspberry liqueur), or other fruit-flavored liqueur
7 oz. white chocolate, chopped
7 oz. heavy cream
1 pt. vanilla or strawberry ice cream
whole strawberries for garnish, optional

Place strawberries, sugar and framboise in a small saucepan over low heat and cook, stirring, for 3 to 4 minutes until the strawberries are beginning to release liquid and the sugar is dissolved. Set aside to cool.

Place chocolate in a glass bowl and microwave on high 1 minute. Stir, and microwave in 30-second increments, stirring after each round, until just melted. Stir until smooth. Whisk in cream until mixture is thick.

Place a scoop of ice cream in each serving dish. Top each scoop with reserved strawberry-framboise mixture. Drizzle white chocolate sauce over top, and garnish with a whole strawberry, if desired.

CHOCOLATE PEAR SUNDAE

Makes 4 servings

Bittersweet chocolate balances the sweetness of pears nicely. The pears and chocolate sauce can be prepared a few days ahead, making this ideal for dinner parties.

2 large pears
1/2 lemon
1/2 cup sugar
2 cups water, divided
1 cup chopped bittersweet chocolate
1/2 cup (1 stick) butter, cut into small pieces
1 pt. vanilla ice cream
1/2 cup slivered almonds, optional

Peel pears, cut in half and core. Rub cut surfaces with lemon to keep pears from browning.

Combine sugar with 1 cup of the water in a medium saucepan and bring to a boil over medium heat, stirring occasionally. When syrup boils and sugar is dissolved, add pear halves, lower heat to medium-low and simmer uncovered, turning pears occasionally, until tender, about 10 minutes. Remove from heat and cool pears in the syrup.

Place chocolate and remaining 1 cup water in a small saucepan over low heat and stir until chocolate is melted and mixture is smooth. Stir in butter a few pieces at a time until melted and sauce is smooth.

Drain pears well. Place a pear half in each serving dish. Top with a scoop of ice cream and drizzle hot chocolate sauce over the top. Garnish with almonds if desired.

SPICY APPLE SUNDAE

Makes 4 servings

Granny Smith apples are perfect in this recipe, but use any tart apple that will hold its shape when cooked. Try the sauce over maple walnut or butter pecan ice cream as well as vanilla.

2 tbs. butter
2 apples, peeled, cored and
  sliced
1/2 tsp. cinnamon
1/4 tsp. ground ginger
1 pinch cloves
2 tbs. packed brown sugar

1/2 tsp. cornstarch
1/3 cup apple juice
1/2 cup heavy cream
1 tbs. sugar
1 pt. vanilla ice cream
12 gingersnap cookies
1/3 cup toasted walnuts, optional

Melt butter in a large skillet over medium heat. Add apples and toss to coat. Sprinkle with cinnamon, ginger, cloves and brown sugar and cook, stirring occasionally, until apples are tender, about 5 minutes. Whisk cornstarch into apple juice and pour mixture into apples in skillet. Cook, stirring, until mixture bubbles and is thick, about 3 minutes. Set aside to cool slightly.

In a small bowl using an electric mixer, beat cream with sugar until soft peaks form. Set aside. (Do this step just before serving.)

Scoop ice cream into 4 serving bowls. Coarsely crumble 2 gingersnaps over each scoop. Spoon warm apple sauce over, and crumble remaining gingersnaps on top. Garnish with whipped cream and walnuts, if desired.

CHERRY-CHOCOLATE SUNDAE

Like a Black Forest cake, this sundae combines cherries and chocolate for a dark, rich sundae.

1 can (16 oz.) black cherries with syrup	1/4 cup heavy cream
2 tbs. unsweetened cocoa powder	1 pt. chocolate ice cream
	1 bar (about 2 oz.) dark chocolate

Drain cherries in a strainer over a bowl. Set cherries aside; place 1/2 cup of the drained syrup (discard remainder) in a small saucepan over medium-low heat. Stir in cocoa powder and cream. Bring to a boil, stirring constantly. Reduce heat to low and simmer until cocoa powder is dissolved and sauce is smooth, about 10 minutes.

Use a vegetable peeler to "peel" curls of chocolate from the chocolate bar. Set curls aside. Place cherries in the bottom of each serving dish. Add a scoop of ice cream and drizzle with sauce. Garnish with chocolate curls.

PEACH-RASPBERRY SUNDAE

Peaches are at their best in the height of summer.

1 1/2 cups fresh or frozen
  raspberries, thawed
juice of 1/2 lemon
3 tbs. sugar, or more to taste

2 tbs. framboise raspberry
  liqueur, optional
2 large peaches
1 pt. peach ice cream

Place raspberries, lemon juice and sugar in a small saucepan over medium-low heat. Bring to a simmer and cook, stirring often, for 5 minutes, until raspberries are soft and sugar is dissolved. Press mixture through a sieve into a bowl, discarding solids. Stir in framboise, if using, and set aside. Fill a large saucepan halfway with water and bring to a boil. Place peaches in boiling water and cook for 2 minutes. Remove peaches, peel and cut in half, discarding pits. Slice each half in 4 pieces. Set aside to cool completely.

Place 2 small scoops ice cream in each serving dish. Top each dish with 4 peach slices, and drizzle with raspberry sauce.

BERRY-CARAMEL SUNDAE

Sweet caramel and tangy berries blend with ice cream for an unforgettable dessert.

1 cup blackberries	3 tbs. sugar
1 cup raspberries	3/4 cup pecans
2 tbs. framboise (raspberry liqueur), or other berry liqueur	1 cup prepared caramel sauce
	1 pt. vanilla ice cream

Place blackberries, raspberries, liqueur and sugar in a bowl and stir to combine. Set aside for 20 minutes. Mash berries with a fork, leaving some whole.

Place pecans in a skillet and toast over medium heat, stirring often, until golden and fragrant. Set aside to cool. Heat caramel sauce in microwave for 1 minute on high until warm. Place a spoonful of berries in the bottom of each serving dish. Top with a scoop of ice cream, drizzle with caramel sauce and remaining berries. Sprinkle with toasted pecans.

APRICOT-PLUM SUNDAE

Whether over strawberry frozen yogurt, lemon sorbet or vanilla ice cream, this fruit topping embodies summer in all its glory. Use peaches if you can't find fresh apricots.

2 tbs. butter
1/4 cup brown sugar, packed
1 pinch ground ginger
2 plums, pitted and sliced

4 fresh apricots, pitted and
   sliced
1 pt. vanilla ice cream

In a large skillet over medium-low heat, melt butter. Stir in brown sugar and ginger. Add plums and apricots and cook, stirring often, until fruit is just tender, about 5 minutes.

Place 1 scoop ice cream in each serving dish. Top with warm fruit sauce.

MEXICAN FRUIT AND TORTILLA SUNDAE

Makes 4 servings

Crisp tortillas dusted with cinnamon sugar provide a south-of-the-border flair to this delectable dessert.

4 flour tortillas (8-inch)
2 tbs. butter, melted
5 tbs. sugar, divided
1 tsp. cinnamon, divided
1 small mango
1/2 cup diced strawberries
1 tsp. lime juice
2 tsp. sugar
1 cup prepared caramel sauce
1 pt. vanilla ice cream

Heat oven to 400°. Line a cookie sheet with foil or parchment paper. Place tortillas on cookie sheet and brush well with melted butter. In a small bowl, stir together 3 tbs. of the sugar with $3/4$ tsp. of the cinnamon; sprinkle mixture over tortillas. Bake until tortillas are crisp and golden, about 5 minutes. Remove tortillas to a rack to cool completely.

Peel and dice mango and combine with strawberries, lime juice and remaining 2 tbs. sugar in a small bowl. Set aside.

Heat caramel sauce in the microwave for 1 minute until very warm; stir in remaining $1/4$ tsp. cinnamon.

Place 1 scoop ice cream in each serving bowl. Top with fruit mixture, then warm caramel sauce. Break tortillas into large pieces and garnish sundaes with them.

MAPLE CRANBERRY SUNDAE

Makes 4 servings

Bring the taste of New England home with this combination of flavors. The tart cranberries mellow the sweetness of the maple syrup. Try to use genuine maple syrup, as it is the star of the show. Sweetened dried cranberries often go by the name Craisins.

1/2 cup walnuts
1 1/4 cups real maple syrup
3/4 cup dried cranberries

1 pinch salt
1 pt. vanilla ice cream

Place walnuts in a small skillet over medium heat and toast, stirring often, until golden and fragrant. Set aside to cool.

In a saucepan over medium-low heat, bring maple syrup to a simmer; reduce heat to low and simmer for 3 to 5 minutes, until slightly thickened. Stir in cranberries and simmer 1 minute longer. Remove from heat and stir in salt; set aside to cool completely.

Place 1 scoop ice cream in each serving bowl and top with sauce and walnuts.

RED, WHITE AND BLUE SUNDAE

A perfect way to ring in the Fourth of July, this patriotic sundae is a big hit with children as well as adults.

1 cup vanilla ice cream
$1/4$ cup coarsely chopped strawberries
$1/4$ cup blueberries
$1/4$ cup marshmallow creme

Place a scoop of ice cream in each serving dish. Top with strawberries on 1 side, blueberries on the other side, and a ribbon of marshmallow creme down the center.

BANANA NUT SUNDAE

Caramelized bananas, toasted coconut, ice cream and nuts combine for a rich and creamy treat.

1/3 cup shredded coconut	1 tsp. lemon juice
1/3 cup chopped macadamia nuts	2 bananas, thickly sliced
2 tbs. butter	1 pt. caramel swirl ice cream
3 tbs. brown sugar	

Place coconut and nuts in a skillet over medium heat and toast, stirring constantly, until they are light golden and fragrant. Transfer to a bowl and set aside to cool. Add butter to same skillet and place over medium heat. When butter is melted, add brown sugar and lemon juice. Stir well, add bananas and cook, stirring often, until sauce is thick and bananas are lightly browned, about 5 minutes.

Spoon half of banana mixture into bottoms of serving dishes. Top each with a scoop of ice cream, then remaining banana mixture, and reserved coconut and nuts.

TROPICAL BERRY SORBET

This refreshing sorbet is a great use for any berries you have stashed in your freezer. A great base for a healthy sundae.

2 cups blueberries
2 cups chopped strawberries
$1/2$ cup cold water

$1/4$ cup frozen pineapple juice
concentrate (not thawed)
1–2 tbs. sugar, optional

Several hours before serving, spread berries in a single layer on a cookie sheet and place in the freezer until frozen. Place frozen berries in locking plastic bags and store in freezer until ready to use. (Can be done up to a month ahead.)

In a large bowl, place frozen berries, water and juice concentrate; stir to combine well. Pour half the berry mixture into a food processor workbowl and process until nearly smooth. Taste and add sugar if necessary. Scrape mixture into a bowl and repeat with remaining berry mixture. Serve immediately, or place sorbet in a container with a tightly fitting lid and freeze for up to 2 days.

TROPICAL FRUIT SUNDAE

Light and refreshing, this is the perfect sundae for a hot summer day — or the dead of winter, when you long for the sun! Omit the rum if serving these sundaes to children.

1/3 cup shredded coconut
1 mango
2 oranges
1 cup pineapple chunks in juice
2 tbs. rum, optional
1 tbs. sugar
1 pt. *Creamy Cantaloupe Sherbet*, page 38, or orange sherbet

Place coconut in a small saucepan or skillet and toast over medium heat, stirring often, until light golden. (You could also toast the coconut in a 350° oven for 8 to 10 minutes.) Set aside.

Peel and pit mango and cut into small chunks; place in a glass bowl. Grate zest from $^1/_2$ of 1 orange and add to mango. Peel both oranges and separate into segments by sliding a knife between the membranes. Reserve juice, and add orange segments and juice to bowl with mangos. Add pineapple with 2 tbs. of pineapple juice to the bowl. Stir in rum, if using, and sugar. Set aside for 15 minutes for flavors to blend. Place a scoop of sherbet in each serving dish. Top with fruit and juices, and garnish with toasted coconut.

CREAMY CANTALOUPE SHERBET

Makes 6 to 8 servings

While this recipe can also be made in an ice cream maker, this method is so simple and delicious. Tuck a few delicate Sugar Cookies, *page 70, into a dish of cantaloupe sherbet as an elegant end to a summer meal. Do use whole milk; skim or low-fat won't produce the same texture.*

1 medium cantaloupe
2 cups whole milk, divided
1/3 cup sugar
1 envelope (1/4 oz.) unflavored gelatin
1/4 cup light corn syrup
1/4 tsp. salt
2 tsp. Midori (melon liqueur), optional

Halve cantaloupe; scoop out and discard seeds. Peel and chop cantaloupe. Place cantaloupe in a food processor workbowl; add 1 cup of the milk. Puree mixture. Refrigerate puree until cold.

Place remaining 1 cup milk in a small saucepan. Stir in sugar and gelatin. Place over low heat and cook, stirring, just until gelatin and sugar dissolve — do not boil. Remove from heat and stir in corn syrup, salt, Midori and cantaloupe puree.

Pour into a metal 9 x 13-inch pan, cover with plastic wrap and freeze for 2 hours, stirring occasionally, until slushy. Place mixture in a food processor workbowl and process about 30 seconds until smooth. Place in a plastic container, press plastic wrap on the surface, and cover with a lid. Freeze until firm, about 4 hours.

RASPBERRY SORBET

Top this fat-free sorbet with curls of bittersweet chocolate for a spectacular finish to a special meal, or over sliced peaches for a healthy summer treat.

6 cups fresh raspberries, or frozen unsweetened raspberries,
  thawed, divided
$^3/_4$ cup sugar, or to taste
$^3/_4$ cup water
1 tbs. lemon juice

Place 5 cups of the berries in a food processor workbowl (in batches if necessary) and pulse until pureed. Press berry puree through a sieve into a bowl. Discard solids. Place remaining 1 cup berries in a small bowl and mash lightly. Stir mashed berries into puree and set aside.

In a small saucepan over high heat, stir together sugar and water. Bring to a boil, reduce heat, and simmer 5 minutes, stirring occasionally. Pour syrup over berry mixture and stir to blend well. Stir in lemon juice.

Pour mixture into a metal 9-inch square pan, cover with plastic wrap and freeze for 2 hours, stirring occasionally, until slushy. Place mixture in a food processor workbowl and process for 30 seconds until smooth. Place in a plastic container, press plastic wrap on the surface, and cover with a lid. Freeze until firm, about 4 hours.

GINGERED PEAR SORBET

This lovely sorbet can be made with ingredients from your pantry. Serve it with a drizzle of chocolate sauce and a few Ginger Crisps, *page 68.*

1 can (29 oz.) pears in heavy syrup
$1/4$ cup sugar
1 tsp. grated fresh ginger
2 tbs. lemon juice
chopped crystallized ginger, for garnish, optional

Drain pears in a strainer over a bowl; set pears aside. Place 1 cup of the pear syrup in a saucepan over medium heat (discard remaining syrup). Add sugar and bring mixture to a boil, stirring constantly. Boil 1 minute or until sugar is dissolved. Stir in ginger and set aside to cool.

Place half the pears in a food processor workbowl and puree. Transfer to a large bowl and repeat with remaining pears. Stir cooled syrup and lemon juice into pureed pears. Pour into a 9 x 13-inch metal pan, cover with plastic wrap and freeze for 2 hours, stirring occasionally, until slushy. Place mixture in a food processor workbowl and process for 30 seconds until smooth. Place in a plastic container, press plastic wrap on the surface, and cover with a lid. Freeze until firm, about 4 hours. Garnish with crystallized ginger, if desired.

TANGERINE SORBET

This sorbet is light and refreshing served with diced fresh fruit.

6 large tangerines
1/2 cup water

3/4 cup sugar
2 tbs. lemon juice

Grate zest from 1 tangerine, taking care to avoid the white pith; set aside. Squeeze juice from all tangerines over a bowl; set aside. You should have about 1 1/2 cups juice. Combine zest, water and sugar in a small heavy saucepan over high heat and bring to a boil. Reduce heat to medium-low and simmer for 20 minutes, stirring occasionally, until syrup is thick and reduced in volume. Set aside to cool.

Pour cooled syrup into a medium bowl. Stir in tangerine juice and lemon juice. Pour into a 9-inch square metal pan, cover with plastic wrap and freeze for 2 hours, stirring occasionally, until slushy. Place mixture in a food processor workbowl and process for 30 seconds until smooth. Place in a plastic container, Cover with plastic wrap, and cover with a lid. Freeze until firm, about 4 hours.

LEMON SORBET

This sorbet is like Italian ice for grownups; try it topped with fresh raspberries. The vodka, while not mandatory, will keep the sorbet soft and creamy, as the alcohol does not freeze.

$3/4$ cup sugar

$3/4$ cup water

$1/2$ tsp. grated lemon zest

$3/4$ cup fresh lemon juice

1 $1/2$ tbs. vodka

Stir together sugar, water and zest in a small saucepan over medium heat. Bring to a boil, stirring often. Reduce heat to low and simmer for 5 minutes. Pour into a large bowl and set aside to cool.

Stir lemon juice and vodka into cooled syrup. Pour into a 9-inch square metal pan, cover with plastic wrap and freeze for 2 hours, stirring occasionally, until slushy. Place mixture in a food processor workbowl and process for 30 seconds until smooth. Place in a plastic container, press plastic wrap on the surface, and cover with a lid. Freeze until firm, about 4 hours.

FRUITY GRANOLA YOGURT SUNDAE

Makes 4 servings

Since the granola can be made ahead (or you could substitute prepared granola), you can whip these up for a quick breakfast or after-school snack.

1 cup rolled oats
1/2 cup shredded coconut
1/2 cup chopped pecans
1/2 tsp. cinnamon
2 tbs. vegetable or canola oil

2 tbs. honey
1 cup diced strawberries
1 cup blueberries
3 cups strawberry yogurt

Heat oven to 350°. In a large bowl combine oats, coconut, pecans, cinnamon, oil and honey. Stir until well mixed. Spread mixture on a cookie sheet and bake about 20 minutes, stirring occasionally, until golden. Set aside to cool, stirring occasionally to break granola up.

In a small bowl, stir together strawberries and blueberries. In each serving dish, alternate layers of fruit, yogurt and granola.

YOGURT-FRUIT SUNDAE

A super-fast and healthy after-school snack that the kids can make themselves.

2 cups seedless grapes (any kind), divided
2 pt. low-fat or fat-free vanilla yogurt, divided
4 graham crackers

Place $1/2$ cup of grapes in each serving bowl. Top with $1/2$ pint of yogurt and crumble a graham cracker on top of each serving.

FROZEN YOGURT-FRUIT SUNDAE

Another variation of this healthy after-school snack that the kids can make themselves. Use any fruit and yogurt they like.

2 cups berries (any kind)
1 tbs. sugar
1 pt. fruit-flavored frozen yogurt
4 cinnamon graham crackers

If using strawberries, slice them. Combine berries and sugar in a small bowl. Place a scoop of frozen yogurt in each serving bowl. Top with berry mixture, then crumble a graham cracker on top of each serving.

ORANGE-BANANA BREAKFAST SUNDAE

Makes 4 servings

For those who aren't grapefruit fans, use tangerines instead (zest and sections), or double up on the oranges.

2 cups low-fat vanilla yogurt
2 oranges
1 large pink grapefruit

2 bananas, sliced
1 tsp. sugar, or more to taste
1 cup favorite cereal, optional

Place yogurt in a medium bowl. Grate zest from 1 orange and $1/2$ of the grapefruit. You should have about 1 teaspoon of each type of zest. Stir zest into yogurt.

Peel oranges, removing all white pith. Section oranges by sliding a knife between the membranes. Repeat with grapefruit. Toss orange and grapefruit sections in a bowl with bananas and sugar.

Place a few spoonfuls of fruit in the bottom of each serving dish. Top with a few spoonfuls of yogurt-zest mixture. Repeat, using remaining fruit and yogurt. Top with cereal, if desired.

STRAWBERRY-VANILLA SUNDAE

Makes 4 servings

Topped with shaved chocolate, this quick and healthy sundae is elegant enough for a dinner party.

1½ cups sliced fresh
  strawberries
3 tbs. sugar, or to taste
1 bar chocolate (about 2 oz.)

1 pt. low-fat vanilla frozen
  yogurt
½ cup chopped walnuts

In a small bowl, combine strawberries with sugar. Stir to mix, and set aside for 5 minutes. Place half the strawberry mixture in a food processor workbowl and puree. Pour pureed strawberries over sliced berries in bowl and stir to combine. Refrigerate until ready to use.

Using a vegetable peeler, "peel" curls of chocolate off the edge of the chocolate bar. Place about 1 tbs. strawberry sauce in the bottom of each serving dish. Top with a scoop of frozen yogurt, and then more strawberry sauce. Garnish with chocolate curls.

HEALTHY SUNDAES

BANANA YOGURT BREAKFAST SUNDAE

Makes 4 servings

A healthy day begins with ingredients like this, yet this dish looks like dessert!

2 bananas
2 cups strawberry-banana or vanilla yogurt
$1/4$ cup wheat germ
1 cup chopped pecans
$1/4$ cup honey
12 raspberries for garnish

Peel and slice bananas, divide among serving dishes and add a spoonful of yogurt atop each serving. Sprinkle with wheat germ and pecans, top with remaining yogurt, and drizzle with honey. Garnish with berries.

CHERRY BLACKBERRY SAUCE

Makes 2 1/4 cups

This is a fabulous sauce when bing cherries are in season. For the rest of the year, use frozen cherries and berries instead, as long as they're unsweetened. Serve this over caramel-vanilla ice cream, over fruit sorbet for a healthy treat, or even over waffles for breakfast.

1/3 cup sugar, or more to taste
1/3 cup water
1 cup (6 oz.) dark cherries, stemmed

1 cup fresh blackberries or frozen blackberries, thawed
2 tbs. butter
1 tbs. lemon juice

In a medium saucepan over high heat, stir together 1/3 cup sugar and water. Bring to a boil, reduce heat to medium, and cook for 5 minutes. While sugar syrup cooks, halve and pit the cherries. Add cherries to syrup and cook over medium heat 2 minutes. Add blackberries and cook 1 minute longer. Taste and add 1 to 2 tsp. sugar if necessary. Remove from heat and stir in butter and lemon juice until incorporated. Serve warm or cold.

BLUEBERRY SAUCE

Makes 1½ cups

Serve a scoop of vanilla or strawberry ice cream on a toasted waffle, and top with this sauce. Frozen blueberries will work fine for this recipe, as long as they're unsweetened.

2 cups fresh blueberries, divided
3 tbs. sugar, or to taste
1 tsp. cornstarch
1 tbs. lemon juice

Place 1¼ cups of the blueberries in a saucepan over medium heat with sugar and cornstarch. Cook, stirring and mashing berries, for 5 to 7 minutes until sauce is thickened and bubbly. Remove from heat and stir in lemon juice and remaining ¾ cup blueberries. Serve warm, or refrigerate in a covered container.

TROPICAL FRUIT AND RUM SAUCE

Makes 6 cups

Pineapple is even sweeter and more intensely flavored when grilled or sauteed. Use canned pineapple (in juice, of course) instead of fresh to enjoy a taste of the tropics any time of year.

1/2 cup diced dried apricots
3 tbs. dark rum, divided
2 bananas
1 tbs. butter
3 cups diced fresh pineapple (1 small), juice reserved
3 tbs. brown sugar
1 tbs. grated fresh ginger
3 tbs. orange juice
1 tsp. cornstarch

Place apricots and 1½ tbs. of the rum in a small saucepan over low heat. Stir well and cover; simmer for 3 minutes, stirring occasionally, until fruit has absorbed most of the rum. Set aside. Peel bananas and chop coarsely; set aside.

Melt butter in a large skillet over medium heat. Add drained pineapple and saute until pineapple is tender and slightly browned, about 5 minutes. Add apricots with liquid, brown sugar, ginger, orange juice and ¼ cup reserved pineapple juice. Bring to a simmer; stir in cornstarch, bananas and remaining 1½ tbs. rum. Simmer, stirring often, until sauce is thickened. Serve warm, or store covered in the refrigerator and reheat just before serving.

RASPBERRY SAUCE

Simple and versatile, this deep red sauce is just as delicious over chocolate ice cream as it is over poached pears.

1 qt. fresh raspberries
1/2 cup raspberry jam or preserves
1 tbs. sugar, optional
1 tbs. framboise (raspberry liqueur), optional

Place raspberries and jam in a food processor workbowl and puree. Taste and add sugar, if needed. Press puree through a strainer into a bowl, discarding solids. Stir in liqueur, if using. Refrigerate until ready to use. Serve cold or at room temperature.

TANGY LEMON SAUCE

Makes ³/₄ cup

Serve this light, lovely sauce over sorbet and berries, or sauteed pears and vanilla ice cream.

¹/₂ cup water
¹/₄ cup sugar
1 tbs. cornstarch
1 tsp. grated lemon zest
3 tbs. lemon juice
1 tbs. butter

Stir together water, sugar, cornstarch and lemon zest in a small saucepan over medium heat. Bring to a boil, reduce heat to medium-low and cook, stirring often, for 5 to 7 minutes until thickened. Remove from heat; stir in lemon juice and butter until butter is melted. Serve warm.

CLASSIC CHOCOLATE SAUCE

Makes about 1 1/4 cups

This is the standard method for making ganache, a versatile chocolate-and-cream mixture. You can thin the sauce, if you wish, with a bit more cream, or skip the extract and add a tablespoon of liqueur or alcohol (rum and brandy are especially good). Remember, the better quality the chocolate, the better the sauce.

1 cup chopped chocolate or chocolate chips
2/3 cup heavy cream
1/2 tsp. vanilla or other flavor extract, optional

Place chocolate in a medium bowl. Place cream in a small saucepan over medium-low heat, and bring to a simmer. Pour hot cream over chocolate. Set aside, uncovered, to melt for 2 or 3 minutes, then stir until sauce is smooth. Stir in vanilla, if using. Serve warm. This sauce can be stored in the refrigerator and reheated over a double boiler or in the microwave.

HOT FUDGE SAUCE

A few minutes of patient stirring over fairly low heat will reward you with a smooth and creamy sauce that's a bit lighter.

¹/₃ cup white sugar
¹/₃ cup brown sugar, packed
¹/₂ cup unsweetened cocoa
  powder

3 tbs. butter
¹/₂ cup heavy cream
¹/₂ tsp. vanilla or other flavor
  extract

In a small bowl, stir together white sugar, brown sugar and cocoa powder; set aside. Melt butter in a small saucepan over low heat. Add cream and raise heat to medium. Cook, stirring constantly, until mixture reaches a simmer (bubbles forming around the edges of the pan). Add cocoa mixture, lower heat to medium-low and cook, stirring constantly, until sugar is dissolved and mixture is thick. Remove from heat and stir in vanilla. Serve hot over ice cream, or store in the refrigerator and reheat over a double boiler or in the microwave.

FAT-FREE CHOCOLATE SAUCE

Guilt-free chocolate sauce can be yours in a matter of minutes. Serve over low-fat vanilla frozen yogurt and garnish with fresh berries for a healthy indulgence.

$1/3$ cup unsweetened cocoa powder
$3/4$ cup sugar
1 tbs. cornstarch
$2/3$ cup evaporated skim milk
$1/2$ tsp. vanilla

Place cocoa powder, sugar and cornstarch in a small saucepan and stir to combine. Stir in evaporated milk and place over medium-low heat. Cook, stirring constantly, for about 10 minutes until sauce is thickened and smooth and sugar has dissolved. Remove from heat and stir in vanilla. Serve warm, or refrigerate until ready to serve and reheat in microwave.

CHOCOLATE ORANGE SAUCE

Makes about 1 cup

A hint of tangy citrus enlivens this fudgy sauce. Serve this over a brownie and a scoop of vanilla ice cream.

3 oz. unsweetened chocolate, chopped
$1/2$ cup brown sugar, packed
$1/3$ cup heavy cream
grated zest of 1 small orange
1 tbs. orange liqueur, optional

Place chocolate, sugar, cream and zest in a small bowl. Pour water to a depth of about 1 inch in a small saucepan, place over low heat and bring just to a simmer. Place bowl with chocolate over the saucepan with simmering water and stir until chocolate is melted, sugar is dissolved and sauce is smooth. Stir in liqueur if using. Serve warm.

CHOCOLATE BUTTERSCOTCH PEANUT BUTTER SAUCE

Makes about 4 cups

With all your favorite candy bar flavors packed into one sauce, this sauce is unbelievably easy to make, and will keep in the refrigerator for a week or so.

2 cups semisweet chocolate chips
1³/₄ cups butterscotch flavored chips
³/₄ cup peanut butter
1 can (12 oz.) evaporated milk

Stir together chocolate chips, butterscotch chips and peanut butter in a large glass bowl. Microwave on high for 1 minute; stir well. Continue microwaving in 30-second increments, stirring after each round, until chips are just melted. Stir until mixture is smooth. Whisk in evaporated milk. Serve warm, or store in the refrigerator and reheat in the microwave.

CARAMEL NUT SAUCE

Try a drizzle of this rich, warm sauce over chocolate ice cream, or with a berry sorbet and enjoy the tart-sweet contrast. Hazelnuts or pecans will work just as well as almonds.

$1/4$ cup ($1/2$ stick) butter

$1/2$ cup slivered almonds

$1/2$ cup brown sugar, packed

$1/2$ cup light corn syrup

2 tbs. water

$1/4$ cup heavy cream

Melt butter in a medium saucepan over medium-low heat. Add almonds and saute, stirring occasionally, until nuts are lightly browned. Remove from heat and stir in brown sugar, corn syrup and water (be careful, as it may bubble up). Return to medium-low heat and cook, stirring constantly, until mixture boils and sugar is dissolved. Carefully stir in cream. Bring to a boil, reduce heat to low, and cook for 5 to 6 minutes longer until sauce is thick. Serve warm, or refrigerate for up to a week and reheat over a double boiler or in a microwave.

CARAMEL PEANUT BUTTER SAUCE

Makes 1¼ cups

This rich and decadent sauce is impossible to resist when served over chocolate ice cream.

½ cup sugar
1 cup heavy cream
¼ cup peanut butter

Place sugar in a heavy medium saucepan over medium heat. Watch sugar until it begins to melt — do not stir! When sugar begins to melt, stir and cook until it turns golden. Watch carefully, as it can burn quickly. Remove pan from heat and carefully stir in cream — it will boil up for a moment. Return to heat and cook, stirring, until smooth. Stir in peanut butter and cook 1 minute longer until smooth. Serve warm over ice cream.

GRANOLA SUNDAE TOPPING

Use this nutty topping on yogurt and fruit for a breakfast sundae, or over a hot fudge sundae for a crunchy surprise. This calls for walnuts, but use any nut you like.

1$^{3}/_{4}$ cups rolled oats
$^{1}/_{2}$ cup brown sugar, packed
$^{1}/_{2}$ tsp. cinnamon
$^{3}/_{4}$ cup chopped walnuts
$^{1}/_{4}$ cup ($^{1}/_{2}$ stick) butter, melted

Heat oven to 350°. In a large bowl, combine oats, brown sugar, cinnamon and walnuts; toss to combine well. Pour melted butter over and toss well to coat. Spread mixture on a cookie sheet and bake for 10 minutes, stirring once. Cool on cookie sheet, stirring occasionally to break up large pieces. Store in the refrigerator in a sealed container when completely cool.

PECAN LACE STRAWS

These thin, crisp cookies are rolled into tubes while hot, and provide a dramatic accent when stuck into a sundae. If you find yourself making these cookies often, purchase a length of thick wooden dowel at the hardware store for wrapping the cookies, or use a really clean broom handle.

1/2 cup sugar
1/2 cup pecans
1/4 cup (1/2 stick) butter, softened
1 tbs. flour
2 tsp. molasses
1 tbs. heavy cream

Heat oven to 350°. Line a cookie sheet with foil and butter the foil. Place sugar and pecans in a food processor workbowl and process until nuts are coarsely chopped. Add butter, flour, molasses and cream and process until a dough forms and nuts are finely chopped (but not ground to a powder). Place level tbs. of dough 3 inches apart on prepared cookie sheet. The cookies spread quite a bit during baking, so you'll need to bake them in batches. Bake for 8 to 10 minutes, until cookies are bubbly and browned. Watch care-fully — they burn easily.

While the cookies are still very warm, roll each one around the handle of a wooden spoon. They will cool and set in just a few minutes. If the cookies cool and stiffen too much to wrap, place them back in the oven for 30 seconds. Slide the wrapped cookies off the handle, and store in 1 layer in a covered container at room temperature.

GINGER CRISPS

Makes about 4 dozen cookies

These spicy cookies add a finishing touch to fruit or caramel sundaes. Try them with Chocolate Pear Sundae, *page 22.*

1 1/2 cups flour
3/4 tsp. cinnamon
1/2 tsp. ground ginger
1/4 tsp. ground cloves
1/4 tsp. nutmeg
1/2 tsp. salt
1/2 tsp. baking soda
3/4 cup (1 1/2 sticks) butter, softened
1 cup brown sugar, packed
1/4 cup molasses
1 egg

Heat oven to 325°. Lightly grease 2 cookie sheets, or line with parchment paper.

In a small bowl, stir together flour, cinnamon, ginger, cloves, nutmeg, salt and baking soda. In a large bowl, using an electric mixer, beat butter until smooth. Beat in brown sugar until light and fluffy. Beat in molasses and egg. Stir in flour mixture until just combined.

Place teaspoonfuls of dough about 1 1/2 inches apart on prepared cookie sheets. Bake for 6 to 8 minutes, or until cookies are lightly browned and slightly cracked on top. Cool completely on a rack before storing at room temperature.

SUGAR COOKIES

Light and crisp, these delicate, buttery cookies complement everything from dense chocolate sundaes to light sorbets. They'll keep for a week at room temperature in an airtight container.

2$\frac{1}{4}$ cups flour
$\frac{1}{2}$ tsp. baking soda
$\frac{1}{2}$ tsp. cream of tartar
1 pinch salt
1 cup (2 sticks) butter, softened
1 cup sugar, divided
$\frac{1}{2}$ cup confectioners' sugar
1 egg
2 tsp. vanilla

Heat oven to 375°. Grease a cookie sheet, or line with parchment paper; set aside.

In a small bowl, stir together flour, baking soda, cream of tartar and salt. In a large bowl, using an electric mixer, beat butter, $1/2$ cup of the sugar, and confectioners' sugar until light and fluffy. Beat in egg and vanilla. Beat in flour mixture just until well combined.

Shape into 1-inch balls and place 2 inches apart on prepared cookie sheet. Place remaining $1/2$ cup sugar in a small bowl. Use the bottom of a drinking glass to press dough balls flat. Sprinkle cookies lightly with sugar.

Bake cookies for about 10 minutes until browned around edges. Cool completely on a rack before storing at room temperature.

BROWNIES

These dense, chocolatey brownies are great on their own, but what brownie isn't improved with a scoop of vanilla ice cream and a dollop of chocolate sauce?

3 oz. unsweetened chocolate, coarsely chopped
1/2 cup flour
1/2 tsp. baking powder
1/2 tsp. salt
1/2 cup (1 stick) butter, softened
1 1/2 cups sugar
3 eggs
1 tsp. vanilla extract
1/2 cup chocolate chips
1/2 cup chopped walnuts, optional

Heat oven to 350°. Grease a 9-inch square pan. Place unsweet-ened chocolate in a small glass bowl and microwave on high for 1 minute. Stir, then microwave in 30-second increments, stirring after each round, until just melted. Set aside.

In a small bowl, stir together flour, baking powder and salt. In a medium bowl, using an electric mixer, beat butter and sugar until light and fluffy. Beat in eggs 1 at a time. Beat in vanilla, then melt-ed chocolate. Stir in flour mixture until just combined. Stir in choco-late chips and nuts, if using. Spread batter in prepared pan and bake for 35 to 40 minutes, until a toothpick inserted in the center comes out with moist crumbs attached. Cool brownies in pan.

LOW-FAT FUDGE CARAMEL BROWNIES

Makes 12 brownies

You will not believe that these treats are low-fat. Top them with a scoop of frozen yogurt and a handful of raspberries, and you have a dessert any restaurant would be proud to serve. Stir flour well and spoon gently into the measuring cups before leveling off.

3 tbs. butter, cut into pieces
1 oz. unsweetened chocolate,
   coarsely chopped
2/3 cup flour
1 cup sugar
1/3 cup unsweetened cocoa
   powder
1/2 tsp. baking powder
1 pinch salt

1 egg
1 egg white
2 tbs. water
1 tsp. vanilla extract
9 chewy caramel squares,
   unwrapped
1 tbs. skim milk
3 tbs. chocolate chips

Heat oven to 350°. Grease a 9-inch square baking pan.

Combine butter and chocolate in a medium glass bowl and microwave on high for 30 seconds. Stir, then microwave in 30-second increments if necessary, stirring after each round, until just melted. Set aside to cool for 5 minutes. In a small bowl, stir together flour, sugar, cocoa powder, baking powder and salt; set aside. Using an electric mixer, beat egg and egg white into chocolate mixture until well combined. Beat in water and vanilla. Stir flour mixture into chocolate mixture until just combined. Spread half the batter in the prepared pan.

Combine caramel candies and milk in a small glass bowl. Microwave on high for 1 minute. Stir, then microwave for 30 seconds longer, if necessary, until just melted. Drizzle melted caramel over batter in pan. Sprinkle with chocolate chips, then gently spoon remaining batter over top. Bake for 30 to 35 minutes or until a toothpick inserted in center comes out with moist crumbs attached. Cool brownies in pan.

CARAMEL GLASS

These stained glass-like pieces of hard caramel candy are simple to make but look as if they came straight from a fancy pastry shop. Stuck in a sundae, they transform ice cream from a casual treat to a dinner party finale. Store at room temperature in an airtight container and they will keep for weeks.

1 cup sugar   ½ tsp. hot water

Line a cookie sheet with foil, and butter the foil well. Set aside. Place sugar in a heavy medium saucepan over medium-high heat. Do not stir, but shake pan occasionally. Once sugar begins to liquefy, reduce heat to medium-low and cook, stirring often, until sugar is completely melted and golden brown. (Watch carefully: sugar can go from golden to burned very quickly.) Remove from heat and immediately stir in hot water. Pour mixture onto prepared cookie sheet and set aside to cool for at least 30 minutes. Break caramel into large pieces.

INDEX